Alice Rossetto

Fish

as it's cooked in

VENICE

Edizioni LA LIBRERIA DI DEMETRA

Editorial coordination: Walter Pedrotti
Paging: Ilaria Stradiotti
Language consuktance: Claudia Marinaro
Photography: Teresa Zille, Archivio Demetra

FISH AS IT'S COOKED IN VENICE
1ⁿᵈ edition August 1998
© DEMETRA S.r.l.
Via Strà, 167 – S.S. 11
37030 Colognola ai Colli (VR)
Tel. 045/6174111 - Fax 045/6174100

• Introduction •

In the Venetian cuisine fish is undoubtedly the boss
and a visit to the beautiful and irresistible
open-air market at Rialto can give us a good idea
of the abundant fishing products with which the city's
cuisine can put itself to the test; pilchards, *peòci*, *granséole*,
cuttlefish large and small, calamari, sardines *de alba*,
anchovies, grey mullet, angler fish, live eel, turbot, dried
salted cod, gilthead, *canòce*, *capeónghe*, scallops, shrimps,
canestrelli, red mullet, bass, *gò* and much, much more.
In a long sequence of possible choices that only by one
glance makes one wish to start cooking.
Even from this point of view Venice is one with the sea,
and its cuisine cannot but be influenced by this fortune,
therefore it is not difficult to find the right dish for every
occasion accompanied by the indisputable bottle of wine
that is able to futher revive the pleasure of being at table.

• How to choose the fish •

It is good to remember that what is known as being fresh fish is the one which is normally bought at the fishmonger's or at the fish market and one presumes that it was caught the night before, without undergoing any procedure of preservation other than being kept at a controlled temperature so as to impede the subsequent natural decomposing process. The quality of fresh fish depends on two fundamental parameters, the period of the year in which it is caught and its state of freshness.

The best period to buy specific species is that which preceeds the laying of the eggs, in which time the meat is richer in phosphorus and is tastier and more delicate. Even the nutritional properties of the fish depend on its quality therefore on its freshness, even the techniques used for fishing can influence these elements.

Once caught if treated with the correct hygenic norms,

conserved in adequate packaging at a temperature slightly above zero and on ice, fish can be considererd edible for about 5 days.

It is obviously adviseable to be able to count on a trustworthy fishmonger on whom one can absolutely rely.

Fresh fish has a shiny skin with metal-like iridescent reflections; the more time passes after catching, the more it looses its characteristics and the skin becomes opaque and therefore becomes of a slimey aspect, with more and more yellowish grey shades. Fresh fish above all has lively eyes, clear and convex; after one or two days after being caught these characteristics begin to vanish, so it is preferable to avoid buying fish with glassy, concave, reddish eyes covered with a whitish film. Lastly, the gills must be red: all shades of red are acceptable, from dull pink to bordeax, but when they begin to turn a brick red, the fish has reached its limit of edibility and if they are brown, it must be thrown away.

Naturally the meat's consistency may vary according to the species and to the size (the larger, the more consistent). A fish that has just been caught has, in any case, a slightly arched, stiff body, phenomenon which lasts according to the fishing methods and preservation. As time passes the fish loses this stiffness and if we then touch its abdomen we will notice that it will have become more or less elastic, then pliable and finally flabby.

Twenty-four hours after catching, fish does not have any particular smell but that of sea and seaweed. Slowly but surely though, it will acquire that typical "fish smell" and then, as time passes,a whole series of smells owing to the decomposition and to the environment in which it is preserved.

The **cephalopod molluscs** when very fresh have a shiny skin with sharp colours and black lively eyes. As time passes the skin becomes opaque and yellowish-grey; if instead they are preserved in ice they acquire at once a white colouring. "Aging", even the eyes become opaque. The odour initially brakish, will quickly lose its sea smell becoming always worse. A minimum of "hanging" is not always to be despised because it makes them softer.

Shelled molluscs must be bought as fresh as possible, preferably live and cooked immediately. An index of their freshness are the valves that must be of an intense colour shiny and well closed or that they close as soon as stimulated. The molluscs in the shells must give off a pleasing and brakish smell, the body must be a vivid colour and well attached to the shell.

Even the **crustaceans** should preferably be bought live or just dead, because they alter very quickly. The colours of the shell must be sharp and shiny; as time passes, the humidity which characterizes them becomes a greyish film. Crustaceans which are not very fresh have limbs and antennas which hang limp as soon as they are lifted; the black and clear eye, slowly but surely becomes opaque and faded, the rosey-white and firm flesh becomes yellowish-grey, then yellow and flabby. Those specimens that when bought have an ammonia smell, symptom of unfreshness, must be discarded.

Most used types of fish	Jan	Feb	Mar	Apr	May	June	July	Aug	Sept	Oct	Nov	Dec
ANCHOVY			*	*	*		*	*			*	
EEL	*	*	*	*	*						*	*
LOBSTER				*	*	*	*	*	*	*	*	*
BASS	*	*				*						
CALAMARI		*	*	*		*	*	*	*	*	*	*
GREY MULLET			*	*	*	*	*	*		*	*	*
MUSSEL		*			*	*	*	*	*	*	*	*
PRAWN				*	*	*	*		*	*	*	*
COD	*	*	*	*	*	*	*	*	*		*	*
GILTHEAD						*	*	*	*	*	*	*
OCTOPUS		*		*	*	*	*		*	*	*	*
SARDINE	*	*	*	*	*	*	*	*	*	*	*	*
CUTTLEFISH		*	*	*		*	*	*	*	*	*	*
RED MULLET	*			*	*	*	*	*	*		*	*
CLAM		*				*	*	*	*	*	*	*

The most indicated periods
to buy certain types of fish.

10

Fish and wine

When the marine world is brought to table, it is so complexed and varied that any type of simplification concerning the matching of wines is useless, but on the whole one can say that to propose a good spumante brut of noteable structure one can never go wrong: and the same can be said for most of the white, young, dry and fruity wines. As for red wines, for certain occasions, some light, young, low tannic, fresh and subtle red wines may result as a excellent matches.

Molluscs in general, especially when eaten as starters or appetizers require white, gentle wines, of moderate alcoholic content and expansive aroma. With calamari, octopus and cuttlefish instead, there are those who prefer the accompanyment of heavier or even rosè wines.

Crustations generally require the great white wines, maybe even a sparkling wine obtained by bottled fermentation, whereas other fish may prefer to be accompanied by different wines, according to the manner in which it is cooked. The gilthead or grey mullet for example, requires wines of certain relevance, whereas fish like eel especially if cooked on the coals may be accompanied by red or rosè wines. With fried fish, it is almost compulsory for one to drink warm, white wines tempered by a decisive acidity and always white but lighter wines even with boiled fish.

**The dosage in the recipes
is to be considered for about four persons.**

• Starters and appetizers •

Compréme co sti bezzi sie grossi de sardelle,
Ma vardè che i ve lassa zernir quelle più belle.
Quella che xe de sora, xe sempre la più grossa,
Quando che le xe stracche, le gh'ha la testa grossa,
Paghéle quel che i altri le paga in pescaria
E po fèvene dar quattro de soravia.

(Carlo Goldoni, *Le donne de casa soa*, 1755)

There is not a tavern, *bàcaro* or Venetian trattoria that does not exhibit its good choice of irresistible appetizers (*cichéti*) with which one can enjoy a glass of wine drunk in company while having a good old chat. It is a tradition that fortunately will find it hard to die, as it is well rooted and conquers even those who just visit the city. The *cichéti* can also be politely proposed as an inviting starter.

• SARDÈE IN SAÓR •
(Pickled pilchards)

600 g of pilchards, 500 g of onions, 1/4 l of wine vinegar, wheat flour as needed, extra-virgin olive oil as needed, salt.

Today *the sardèe in saór*, quite a well known dish, is eaten as a whim and appetizing starter. The ancient habit of marinating foods with onion is most probably tied to the life of seafaring people; it would in fact be used to conserve some foods and consume them during the course of long sea voyages. The pilchards must be prepared at least two days earlier before serving and must be left to rest in a fresh place, so that they may become enriched with flavour; a patient wait of a week will allow you to taste them at their best.

Get yourself some very fresh pilchards, discard the heads and the intestines, wash, dry, flour and fry them in a pan with abundant extra-virgin olive oil. Then transfer them onto a sheet of absorbent kitchen paper and salt them.

Peel and cut the onions into very fine rings and let them brown slowly in another pan with oil, stirring them continuously with a wooden spoon, in such a way that they brown without burning and become very tender and transparent. Add the vinegar and, as it starts boiling, take the pan off the flame and leave to cool.

Lay on the bottom of a terracotta bowl not treated with toxic paints, a layer of fried pilchards, cover them with a layer of onions and continue to alternate a layer of pilchards with a layer of onions, also using the cooking gravy.

Put them in a fresh place and let the flavour mature for at least a couple of days; at the moment you serve them, open a bottle of rosè wine.

If you feel like trying some variant of this famous recipe, keep in mind that the habit of adding raisins and/or some pine seeds during the cooking of the onions is quite wide-spread. This will allow you to obtain a type of sweet and sour that could result in being very appetizing. The pine seeds or raisins, washed and soaked in a little warm water could instead be added at the moment when you layer the pilchards and onions.

• SARDÓNI CÓ 'L PARSÉMOLO •
(Pickled anchovies)

*500 g of very fresh anchovies, 1 l of vinegar of white wine
1 lemon, 2 bay leaves, 1 small bunch of parsley,
extra-virgin olive oil, salt.*

Clean the anchovies discarding the heads and the spinal bone (you should be able to remove both with one single movement), wash them and dry them by lying them on a dish towel. Arrange them in a glass or ceramic container with high sides and season with the grossly chopped bay leaves, the lemon peel (only the yellow part) and the parsley.

Then cover them with previously boiled vinegar and leave them to ferment.

After about four hours drain the anchovies and lay them in

another ceramic container with high sides, salt and cover them with a slight layer of olive oil and they are ready to be consumed.

• SCHIE AGIO E OGIO •
(Lago on shrimps and garlic)

700 g of lagoon shrimps, 1/2 lemon, 2 garlic cloves, extra-virgin olive oil, 1 bunch of parsley, salt.

With the grey, typical lagoon shrimps, called schie in dialect (maybe from the Greek word skià, shadow), a very appetizing starter is prepared, that can obviously also be used as an irresistable *cichéto*. They can be prepared in various ways.

Carefully wash the shrimps under running water and then pour them into a large pot in which you will have boiled some water, salted and acidulated with lemon juice. After about 3 minutes, as soon as a light foam starts to form, drain, patiently peel, place in a bowl or onto a serving dish and flavour them with an emulsion prepared with oil, chopped parsley and salt. If you so desire, finally serve them with maize porridge (*polenta*) that you have prepared in the meantime and, of course, with a good bottle of fresh, sweet, dry, white wine.

• CAPEÓNGHE IN TÉCIA •
(Razor - clams in the pan)

1 kg of razor-clams, 2 garlic cloves, 8 spoons of extra-virgin olive oil, 1 small bunch of parsley, salt.

Capeónghe, also called *cape da déo*, are characteristic long, tubular, yellow/brown coloured shells of about 10 cm in length, that can also be eaten raw as long as you are sure of their origin and their freshness.

They burrow in the sands along the shore and traditionally are caught in the early morning on the beaches or simply bought at the fish market, as they are cultivated in special basins. As for the preparation of this easily made and very tasty dish, proceed as follows.

First of all wash the clams very well under running water so as to eliminate the residue sand. Then fry some garlic cloves and chopped parsley in a pan, add the razor-clams, discard the garlic and leave it on the flame for about 10 minutes.

After the given time, take the molluscs from the valves and put them on a hot serving dish, leaving the bottom of the pan sandy. Finally season with salt, serve with some slices of toasted bread and some good, fresh, dry, white wine.

• SCHIE FRITE •
(Fried lago on shrimps)

700 g of lagoon shrimps, maize seed oil, salt.

Lagoon shrimps can also be served fried and in that case it is not necessary to shell them. After having washed them under cold water and carefully drained them, fry them in abundant oil and take them out of the pan and leave them for a moment to dry on some absorbent kitchen paper before transferring them onto a suitable serving dish and serve them with good, steaming, maize porridge (polenta). It is necessary to accompany it with a good, dry, white wine.

• CANÒCE LÉSE •
(Boiled mantis shrimps)

750 g of mantis shrimps, extra-virgin olive oil as needed,
the juice of 1/2 lemon, one small bunch of parsley,
salt, pepper.

Mantis shrimps are crustaceans with very delicately flavoured meat, they are very popular in Venice and sought-after towards the end of November when they are richer in flesh - so much so that they are subject to a saying that goes: *"De santa Caterina na canòcia val na gaìna"* (On the day of Saint Catherine, 25th November, a *canòcia* is worth as much as a chicken). The preparation of this recipe is very simple.

● SCHIE FRITE ●
(Fried lagoon shrimps)

After having washed the mantis shrimps pour them into a pot of salted boiling water and leave them for 5-6 minutes. Then drain and let cool.

Now the relatively more difficult part of the recipe begins. Unless you decide to serve them as they are, leaving the task of opening the shrimps to each guest. Peel them taking off the heads and cut them with a small pair of scissors along the border, on the tail and under the head so as to keep only the body. Lay them one by one on a suitable serving dish and flavour them with a mixture of oil, lemon juice, salt and pepper, finally complete with finely chopped parsley. Serve with fresh white wine.

Keep in mind another variant concerning the use of mantis shrimps: after boiling you can cut them in half longwise, passing them through wheat flour and dipping them in salted beaten egg and then grated bread, lastly brown them in butter.

MANTIS SHRIMPS IN BROTH

Using the head, the legs and the carapace of the mantis shrimps, obtained from the cleaning operation of the crustaceans, you can make an excellent fish broth that can be used for the preparation of various recipes. Pour it all into the broth and boil it again adding about 1/2 a glass of white wine for every 1/2 kg of mantis shrimps. After boiling them for about 20 minutes, let it cool and scrape to recuperate all the possible pulp, gather the juices and filter the broth.

LUNGHEZZE MINIME PERMESSE
PER LA VENDITA DEL PESCE
DELLE SEGUENTI QUALITÁ

CENT.

BARBON. TRIA. SARDELLA. SARDON 7

BRANZIN. ORADA. DENTAL. CORBO ⎫
SPARO. BOTOLO. BOSEGHETA. SOASO ⎬ 12
LOTREGAN. MECIATO. VERZELATA ⎪
LOVO. SFOGIO. PASSARIN. ROMBO ⎭

BISATO.   25

OSTREGA.   5

PEOCIO.   3

Plaque of minimum lengths permitted
for the selling of fish at the Rialto market.

• FOLPÉTI CÓNSI •
(Small flavoured octopuses)

12 small octopuses, 6-7 spoons of extra-virgin olive oil,
1 lemon, salt, pepper.

It is a starter or an appetizer which is simply and rapidly prepared: the important thing is to get some small, fresh octopuses. After having cleaned them let them cook in a pot of boiling water until adequately tender. Then drain them, cut them in half lenghthwise and place them onto a serving dish. Finally season them with lemon juice, salt and pepper, decorate all around with sprigs of parsley and serve with a bottle of good fresh, white wine (a *Tocai di Lison*, as also a *Chardonnay*, will certainly make a good impression).

• GARÙSOI CÓNSI •
(Flavoured sea snails)

1,2 kg of sea snails, 2 cloves of garlic, extra-virgin olive oil,
3 spoonsful of wine vinegar, 1 small bunch of parsley,
a few lemon peels, salt, pepper.

First of all get some very fresh sea snails, wash them carefully under running water and drop them into a pot of cold water, add the lemon peels, the vinegar and a bit of salt, place it on the fire, bring the water to the boil and let them cook on a moderate flame for about 3/4 of an

● FOLPÉTI CÓNSI ●
(Small flavoured octopuses)

hour if they are "young" specimens (distinguished by their light colour) and for 1 hour if they are "old" specimens (dark coloured).

After the necessary cooking time has passed, drain the garùsoi and, using a toothpick or a suitable pin, extract the flesh from every snail and discard the most leathery part, the one which remains in contact with the air.

Lastly season with a mixture of chopped garlic and parsley, oil, salt and pepper, let them cool well and serve with a fresh, dry, white wine or, if you prefer, with a not too heavy, red wine.

• CAPESANTE AL FORNO •
(Baked scallops)

8 large scallops, 1 glass of dry white wine, 20 g of butter,
1 spoon of extra-virgin olive oil, 1 spoonful of brandy
1 clove of garlic, a few sprigs of parsley,
1 pinch of origanum, grated bread as needed, salt, pepper.

The scallop, also called "St. James's shell", is a typical fan shaped shell in which the mollusc has a firm flesh (the best period for it to be eaten is from September to May). The necessary operations to take the molluscs out require a little patience, but they can be faced with total ease.

Brush and wash every shell carefully and then, using a kitchen towel, keep it firmly in the left hand, in such a way that the flat shell is facing upwards and the joining point of the two valves is facing outwards.

With your right hand stick a small knife in a crack between the two valves and with a jerking movement force, without breaking, moving up to the joining point and cutting the muscles that keep the mollusc anchored to the shell. If this operation is impossible, put the shell into the oven at a moderate temperature, so that the valves may open without difficulty.

Once the shells are open, let the blade slip underneath the external, greyish border (the "cloak") to detach the mollusc. Divide the "nut" (white mussel) and the coral from the rest that is to be discarded, eventually conserving the "cloak", that can be used for broth or fish fumé.

Rinse the molluscs under water, dry them, dip them in grated bread and place them in a saucepan; add the wine, the butter, the oil, the brandy, the peeled and chopped garlic together with the parsley, the origanum, salt and pepper, complete with a couple of a glasses of water and place in the oven at medium temperature for more or less 10 minutes. Meanwhile clean the upper shells of the scallops well, heat them and when the scallops are ready, put one in each shell, pour some of the juice from the cooking onto them and serve on a suitable plate, with salad in season and a good bottle of fresh, white wine, a *Prosecco* or a *Tocai di Lison*.

HOLY SCALLOPS!

The scallops or shells of St. James are so called because it is beleived that in the Middle Ages they were gathered off the Spanish Galician coast, where they were used, after being deprived of their edible parts, as a symbol for the pilgrims who journeyed to a place called Santiago de Compostela, believed to be the burial place of James the Apostle, that attracted visitors from every part of Europe, Italy included. A very widespread medievel legend spoke of a young man travelling with his family to the Compostela Sanctuary where he would have prayed in presence of the mortal remains of St. James. The boy had been unjustly accused by a young girl whom he did not love, he was condemned to be hanged. The parents who left him as he was about to alight the platform, came back to the place of execution, after their pilgrimage of 36 days and miraculously found the boy still alive. St. James had knelt beneath him preventing him from suffocating.

• Sepioìne aea grèa •
(Small grilled cuttlefish)

500 g of small cuttlefish, 1 lemon not treated with surface preservatives, parsley, extra-virgin olive oil.

Clean some small and tender cuttlefish well, wash and let them cook on a grill for just 5 minutes, brushing them with a little oil. Then serve them very hot, sprinkled with finely chopped parsley and grated lemon peel (use only the yellow part) and accompany them by a bottle of adequately chilled, dry, white wine, a *chardonnay* perhaps.
If you haven't a grill cook the cuttlefish in the oven.

• Granséola có 'l limón •
(Lemon granceola "crab")

*4 granceola of medium size (about 300 g each),
less than 1/2 glass of extra-virgin olive oil,
1 small bunch of parsley, salt and pepper.*
<u>For completion:</u> *salad, small anchovies, small lemon slices, hard boiled eggs.*

The *granséola* (granceola or grancevola) is a large type of crab typical of the Venetian lagoon. It hasn't much meat, but it is lean and of an intense flavour; the pulp is mainly in the legs but the liver and the creamy substance under the shell is not to be discarded.
The preparation is not difficult, but requires a great deal

of patience when taking the pulp out of the shell and the legs. The best period to be eaten is in autumn, between October and December. Carefully wash the *granséole*, brush the shell with a small metal brush and let simmer in salted water for about 20 minutes. Drain and leave them to cool. Then start opening every *granséola* to recuperate the flesh. Take the upper part of the cuirass with the right hand and, while still holding the lower part with the left hand, detach the back from the legs. Extract and keep the coral aside, it is very rare and can be used other than for flavouring this recipe, also for preparing composite butter and accompanying sauces.

Clean the legs taking off the meat that may have remained attached to the cartilage and crush it with a pestle, nutcracker or special pliers, so as to extract the pulp contained inside. Treat the claws likewise.

A mass of white flesh will remain attached to the shell and is easily detachable: taking care to get rid of all the spongy and undigestible parts and pass it through the sieve.

Then unite all the obtained pulp, carefully wash the cuirass and cover the inside with a salad leaf. Lay the pulp on top of it and flavour with a sauce prepared with oil, lemon juice, salt and pepper. If you wish, you may decorate it with small slices of lemon, small anchovies and hard-boiled egg medallions.

Serve together with some fresh, white wine, a *Tocai di Lison* or a *Prosecco* for example, to be opened at 10 °C.

● GRANSÉOLA CÓ 'L LIMÓN ●
(Lemon granceola "crab")

• Bacaeà Mantecà •
(Creamed salted cod)

600 g of soaked and boned salted cod,
extra-virgin olive oil as needed, 1 clove of garlic,
1 small bunch of parsley, salt, pepper.

Creamed salted cod is served cold, not only as a starter but as a second course and is unfailingly served with maize porridge (*polenta*) and can be prepared beforehand. The good outcome of this recipe depends on the patience and the ability with which the salted cod is transformed into a fluffy cream.

After having washed it put the cod into a pot of water, bring it to the boil and leave it to boil on a moderate flame for about 40 minutes.

Then drain the fish, discard the skin and reduce the pulp to minute pieces, put them in a pan and beat them with a wooden spoon, together with the oil poured in a little at a time, so that, slowly but surely, it may become a thick white cream, where the pieces of cod have become nearly pulverised thanks to the incessant and energic beating.

Continue adding oil until the mixture becomes saturated and then add to the cream salt, freshly ground pepper and a mixture of chopped garlic and parsley.

Lastly serve on a serving dish, accompanying it with some slices of yellow maize porridge (*polenta*), browned on the grill on which you will eventually be able to spread the cod cream. A white *Tocai di Lison* freshly uncorked will be an excellent match.

• Bisàto cóea salsa •

(Eel in sauce)

2 eels of about 600 g, salt.
For the sauce: 3 salted anchovies, 1 egg, 1 clove of garlic,
2 glasses of extra-virgin olive oil, white vinegar,
2-3 bread rolls, 1 small bunch of parsley, pepper.

First of all prepare the sauce. Hard boil an egg and in the meantime crumble the inner part of the bread rolls and wet it with vinegar until it is well soaked.

Gate at the market of Rialto:
PISCIS, PRIMUM A CAPITE FOETET

Without rinsing them under water, carefully clean the salt off the anchovies, bone and crush them into a paste in a mortar, mixing them with the yolk of a hard boiled egg. Then emulsify the anchovy paste with two glasses of oil added slowly, add the finely chopped parsley and garlic and the soft inner part of the bread rolls squeezed free of the vinegar, using a pestle as a spoon or replacing it with a wooden spoon.

Sprinkle it with ground pepper.

You should obtain a sauce of a semi fluid consistency but if not so, add more oil.

Now start with the eels. Clean them and without skinning, cut them into pieces of about 5 cm in length, salt and place on the grill of a hot oven. Grill for 5 minutes at 220 °C, then lower the temperature to 170 °C and finish grilling (it should take about 15 minutes). To prevent the fat of the eel dripping on the tray of the oven producing smoke and giving the fish a bitter taste, cover the tray with a film of water. Once you have finished cooking, place the pieces of eel onto a serving dish, flavour them with the sauce and serve hot.

THE DIFFICULTY OF CLEANING EELS

Usually in recipes that concern the cooking of eels in the oven on the grill it is preferable not to eliminate the skin of the fish, that can eventually be discarded when it has lost its fat; the cooking of eel with its skin allows it to maintain its flavour and tenderness.

However, the skin must be well cleaned before cooking, traditionally it was the habit rub it with some coarse salt, maize flour or grated bread. In case one wants to eliminate it before cooking, one must first take into account its sliminess which does not allow a good grip. See that you hold the eel tightly with the help of a kitchen towel or rubbing it as suggested above.

Hold the eel on the work space so that its back faces up and with a small, sharp knife cut a ring under its head and delicately lift the flap of skin. With the left hand anchor the eel by the head and with the right hand and a kitchen towel take the flap and pull it along the body: if you prefer to hang the eel by the head on a hook instead, with a decisive tug, pull the skin downwards towards the tail, in this way the skin comes off perfectly.

Once the skin is eliminated, cut off the head and cook the eel according to the recipe, cutting it into pieces that will be firstly washed and dried.

The skin of small eels can instead be eaten.

• BISÀTO IN CÓNSA •
(Pickled eel)

1 eel about 800 g, 1 onion, 1 celery stalk,
1 carrot, 1 clove of garlic, 2 bay leaves, 1 l of wine vinegar,
extra-virgin olive oil, wheat flour, pepper in granules.

Clean and skin the eel, cut it into sections of about 8 cm in length and, after slightly flouring, fry it in abundant boiling oil. Then let it dry on some absorbent kitchen paper and keep it warm.

Meanwhile clean and grossly cut the vegetables and let them fry in a couple of spoons of oil for about 20 minutes. Now and then add a little hot water so that they do not become too hot and after about ten minutes of cooking add the vinegar and let it evaporate to a third.

Finally lay the eel in a large sided container of glass or ceramic and season it with pepper in granules, the vegetables and the boiling vinegar. As soon as it has all cooled to room temperature, leave it to rest for a few days in the coolest part of the refridgerator before serving.

• Fish and pasta •

Comparse el gran Sturion
Insieme co del Ton
Trutte, Carpioni, e Rombi,
Varioli, Lizze, e Scombri,
Lucerne e Barboni
Pesce Spada, Anguiloni,
Lamprede con morona,
E Tarantella bona,
La Sardella del Lago:
E po l'occhietto trago,
A Seppe soffegae
Suri, dentali, e orae,
Soasi, e Lattesioli
Alboir, ragni e sardelle,
Passere, e robe belle.

(from *La Bagozzeide*, dedicated to Missier Alvise Pisani
in the year 1733)

Traditionally the pasta in Venice - like in all of Veneto - was prepared at home. The *bìgoi*, quite large pasta, was obtained from dark wholewheat flour, through the use of a special household press equipped with a cylinder that used to make a type of large spaghetti come out from its punctured bottom. This instrument is quite easy to use but requires a certain amount of strength. It is still in use especially in some areas of the hinterland even though mainly white flour is used. In any case, if you do not have the real *bìgoi* you can rely some good spaghetti, preferably the large type. The traditional condiments lend themselves well as far as flavouring goes.

• BÌGOI IN SALSA •
(Bigoli in sauce)

400 g of bìgoi, *or large spaghetti, 100 g of salted pilchards,*
2 medium sized onions, 6 spoons of extra-virgin olive oil,
salt, pepper.

Pilchard sauce which is prepared without any difficulty and does not require any complicated operations, gives pasta a very particular and decisively appetizing flavour. The best result would be obtained if the *bìgoi* were to be made at home as it was once done, preferably using wholemeal or semi refined flour (type 1 or 2), but if you do not want to complicate matters you can use ready-made pasta possibly bought in a shop for homemade foods. Once the *bìgoi in salsa* "was a must" for the Easter eve dinner, as for every Friday and Ash Wednesday; they in fact allowed one to abstain from eating meat and animal fat.

Peel the onions, slice them finely and brown them in oil, mixing them with a wooden spoon and adding a few spoons of water so that they do not darken. Add the cleaned scaled and desalted pilchards without washing them, stir, season with some ground pepper and lower the flame, leaving it to cook on a moderate flame until the pilchards are nearly disintegrated.

Meanwhile put a pot of water on the flame, bring it to the boil, salt slightly and put in the pasta. Let it cook until ready and then drain carefully, pour it into a soup tureen and flavour it with the sauce, mixing well.

Serve with a white wine, a freshly opened *Tocai di Lison* for example.

• BÌGOI CÓEA RÈNGA •
(Bigoli with herring)

400 g of bìgoi *or spaghetti, 200 g of smoked herring fillets,
250 g of peeled tomatoes, 2 spoons of extra-virgin olive oil,
1 clove of garlic, a few sprigs of parsley,
salt, pepper.*

Rénga da vòvi, with eggs, and *rénga da late*, with milk: the first male and the latter female, used in the preparation of a few typical and popular dishes, so much so that even today the story is told of when decades ago in poor families it was the habit to hang a *rénga* up as a "lamp", so that the diners could flavour their maze porridge (*polenta*) by touching the herring, and in this way not consuming it normally, it could last much longer.

Using a small saucepan, heat the oil and add the whole, peeled clove of garlic: when it has browned take it out and add the tomatoes, squeezed with a fork. Then wash the parsley and add it to the tomatoes, flavour with a pinch of salt and some ground pepper and leave to cook on a fairly lively flame for five minutes.

Meanwhile finely chop the herring and add it to the sauce, lower the flame and continue cooking for about half an hour, until the sauce has adequately thickened.

Then put the pot for the pasta on the fire, when the water boils, salt it and put the *bìgoi* or the spaghetti in. Cook them "al dente", drain them, pour them into a soup tureen and finally flavour with the herring sauce. After having mixed it well serve with a bottle of good, fresh white wine, a classical *Tocai di Lison* for example.

• BÌGOI CÓ SARDÓNI DE ALBA •
(Bigoli with anchovies)

400 g of bìgoi *or spaghetti, 200 g of very fresh anchovies,*
400 g of grated bread, 2 cloves of garlic, 1 small bunch
of parsley, 4 spoons of extra-virgin olive oil,
the juice of 1/2 a lemon, salt.

De alba: which means 'caught at dawn'. It is in this way that the fishmongers of the Rialto fish market describe anchovies or other fish when they wish to highlight the particular freshness.

The anchovy sauce is prepared with a few and cheap ingredients. It requires a little hard work with regards to the cleaning of the fish but it is not such a complicated matter as to create great difficulties. If you are not able to obtain some good and traditional *bìgoi* use spaghetti as long as they are large enough.

Then clean the anchovies eliminating the heads, the tails and the spines, carefully wash the fillets under running water, grossly chop them and place them in a casserole with a mixture of chopped parsley and garlic, the grated bread and the oil. Leave for a few minutes on quite a lively flame mixing with a wooden spoon, until the anchovies are tender and the grated bread browned.

At this point put the pot for boiling the pasta on the flame and when the water starts boiling, salt it and put in the bìgoi or spaghetti. Let them cook "al dente", then stir and transfer the pasta to a soup tureen; sprinkle it with filtered lemon juice, mix it carefully and lastly flavour it with the anchovy sauce, mix it again and serve it without hesitation, not forgetting a bottle of good, fresh, white wine: a *Tocai di Lison* will certainly not be unappreciated.

• SPAGHETI CÓE SÉPE •
(Spaghetti with cuttlefish)

400 g of spaghetti, 500 g of small cuttlefish, 1 onion,
1/2 a stalk of celery, 1 small carrot, 1 small bunch of parsley,
1 sprig of rosemary, 1/2 glass of extra-virgin olive oil,
salt, pepper.

Clean the cuttlefish by eliminating the bone, the eyes and the ink intestines. Carefully wash them, separate the intestines from the sacs, cut the first in small pieces and the rest into strips. Pour the oil into a pan, heat it and add a mixture of chopped onion, celery, carrot, rosemary and the tentacles in pieces. Let them soften, then add the rest of the cuttlefish and, after seasoning it with salt and pepper, bring it to cook on quite a moderate flame, adding a few spoons of warm water if necessary. Lastly complete with some chopped parsley.

Meanwhile boil the water for the pasta, salt it and put in the spaghetti. Cook them "al dente", drain them, tranfer them to a soup tureen and flavour them with the cuttlefish sauce. Serve with some fresh, dry, white wine, choose between a *Tocai*, a *Riesling* or a *Pinot grigio*.

• SPAGHETI CÓE CANÒCE •
(Spaghetti with mantis shrimps)

350 g of spaghetti, 500 g of canòce, 1 clove of garlic,
4-5 peeled tomatoes, 3 spoonsful of extra-virgin olive oil,
7 basil leaves, 1/2 lemon, salt, pepper in granules,
powdered red pepper.

Carefully wash the mantis shrimps under running water, put them into a pot and cover them with moderately salted water. Add the lemon and some pepper in granules, bring to the boil and let them cook for just 3 minutes, take it off the flame and let it cool.

After about half an hour, take the *canòce* out of the pot, take off their head and legs and, using a scissors, open each one's cuirass so as to extract the edible part. Then put back the heads and cuirasses into the pot and once more bring it to the boil. Meanwhile pour the oil into a pan, heat it and fry the garlic before adding the peeled tomatoes cut into small pieces, leave it to cook on a moderate flame, stirring now and then with a wooden spoon, flavouring as needed with some powdered red pepper.

While the sauce is on the flame, filter the water that was used to cook the *canòce*, add some more water to it, boil it again and use it to cook the pasta.

Lastly unite the pulp of the *canòce* to the tomato sauce, complete with the finely chopped basil leaves and leave it to cook for a few minutes. When the spaghetti are done, drain them and flavour them with the sauce, mix carefully and serve together with some fresh, white wine.

• TAJADÈE CÓE CAPESANTE •
(Tagliatelle with scallops)

400 g of tagliatelle, 12 scallops, 120 g of butter,
1/2 glass of dry vermouth, 2 dl of fish fumè,
1 dl of dry white wine, 1 dl of cooking cream, 1 green onion,
1 clove of garlic, 1 small bunch of parsley, salt, pepper.

Clean the green onion, chop it finely and make it soften by putting it on the flame together with the wine and the fish fumet. Let the liquid evaporate until half on a moderate flame. Lengthen it with the cream and, without stopping to stir make it thicken maintaining a low flame. Combine with the cream 100 g of butter left to soften to room temperature and cut into small pieces, then salt, pepper it and take it off the flame, keeping the sauce hot.

Open the scallops and seperate the molluscs from the valves; clean and cut them in two. Flavour the left-over butter with the pressed garlic clove, then discard the latter and fry the scallops in the butter; after a couple of minutes wet them with the vermouth and let it evaporate almost completely. Lastly season with salt and pepper, sprinkle with chopped parsley turn the flame off and keep hot.

Put the pot for the pasta on the flame, when the water starts to boil salt it, put the tagliatelle in and cook them "al dente". Then drain, pour them into a soup tureen and flavour them the butter sauce and garnish with the scallops. Do not forget to serve with a bottle of good wine preferably with a rosé or a fresh white wine.

● TAJADÈE CÓE CAPESANTE ●
(Tagliatelle with scallops)

• TAJADÈE CÓE SÉPE E I PEÒCI •
(Tagliatelle with cuttlefish and mussels)

350 g of tagliatelle, 250 g of cuttlefish,
200 g of peòci (mussels), 1/2 an onion,
less than 1/2 glass of extra-virgin olive oil,
1/2 glass of dry white wine, 200 g of peeled tomatoes,
1/2 a yellow, green pepper, salt, pepper.

First of all clean the cuttlefish, taking off the ink sacks and carefully keeping them aside. Then cut them into small strips.

Peel the onion, finely slice it and fry it in a saucepan with half the oil. Add the cuttlefish, let them fry for a few minutes, wet them with wine, let it evaporate, add the small ink sacks and the peeled tomatoes squashed with a fork. Continue cooking on a moderate flame, cover it with a lid and mixing now and then with a wooden spoon.

Meanwhile clean the green pepper, cut it into small thin strips and stir fry it in a pan with the remaining oil.

After a few minutes of cooking add the mussels and let them cook on a moderate flame for 10 minutes.

Then pour the mussels and green peppers into the casserole in which you cooked the cuttlefish, season with salt and pepper and let it cook on a moderate flame for a few minutes, mixing with a wooden spoon so that the flavours may adequately amalgamate.

In the meantime put a pot of water on the cooker, bring it to boil, salt it and drop in the tagliatelle. Leave them to cook "al dente" carefully drain them and flavour them with the mussel and cuttlefish sauce.

Do not forget to serve this dish with a bottle of good, fresh white wine, a *Tocai di Lison* or a *Riesling* for example, excellent for the greater enjoyment of this dish.

• TAJADÈE CÓI BARBONI •
(Tagliatelle with red mullet)

350 g of tagliatelle, 750 g of red mullet,
200 g of peeled tomatoes,
1 medium sized carrot, 1 celery stalk, 1 clove of garlic,
8 spoons of extra-virgin olive oil,
1 glass of dry, white wine, 1 bay leaf, salt.

Wash the red mullets, clean them carefully, remove the scales, open them in half and patiently remove the bones. Then clean the carrot and the celery, wash, dry and chop them finely.

Using a casserole with reasonably high sides put in the

chopped vegetables and the pressed garlic, add half the oil, salt and cover, leaving to cook on a very moderate flame for about 10 minutes, stirring now and then and adding, if necessary, some spoons of hot water. When the vegetables are tender take off the lid, increase the heat, add the red mullet pulp and stir again.

Then wet with white wine, let it evaporate and add the bay leaf and the peeled tomatoes leaving it to cook on a lively flame, so that the water of the tomatoes may rapidly evaporate. Lastly add salt.

Put a pot of water on the fire and, when it has begun to boil, salt and drop the pasta in. Cook "al dente", drain it well, pour it into a soup tureen, flavour with the remaining oil and finally with the sauce.

Serve immediatly with a fresh, white wine: a *Tocai di Lison* will make a good impression.

• Fish and rice •

> *Uno loda el bisato, un altro el ton;*
> *Quelo porta la rasa e questo el go;*
> *Qua se esalta l'orada e là el barbon;*
> *Chi preferisse el rombo e chi l'nchiò;*
> *El molo Caio vol, Tizio el sardon,*
> *Ma, in fazza de chiunque, mi dirò*
> *Ch'el pesse, che dev'esser più stimà*
> *Per tutte le raxon, xe el Bacalà.*

(Luigi Plet, *El bacalà*, 1850)

Rice, a cereal which has found its ideal terrain for cultivation in the Po valley, has slowly allowed the selection of different varieties for multiple cooking purposes, finds its use in the preparation of some typical Venetian dishes. Thanks to the fact that its cultivation has developed by using water the combination with seafood products has been very successful.

• Risi e sepioìne •
(Rice with small cuttlefish)

300 g of rice, 350 g of small cuttlefish, 1/2 l of meat broth,
40 g of butter, 4 spoons of extra-virgin olive oil,
1/2 onion, 1 clove of garlic, 1/2 glass of dry, white wine,
a few sprigs of parsley, salt, pepper.

First of all dedicate some time to the cleaning of the cuttlefish, eliminating the eyes, bone and the beak. Being very careful not to break them, put away half of the ink sacs - used by cephalopod molluscs to intimidate their aggressors -, eliminating those that seem harder and more granulous to the touch. Then wash the cuttlefish under running water and dry them.

Pour the oil into a casserole, add the butter keeping a knob aside and fry the cleaned, finely sliced onion and the cleaned garlic left whole. When the clove of garlic has browned, eliminate it and pour the cuttlefish and the ink sacs left aside, into the container, season with salt and pepper. Then lower the flame and let it simmer at a moderate heat adding white wine a little at a time and cover with a lid.

When the sauce has thickened, pour the rice into the casserole and let it cook, stirring with a wooden spoon and adding the broth a little at a time.

When it is ready, complete with a knob of butter and the chopped parsley, serve with a bottle of good, fresh, white wine, a *Tocai di Lison* or a *Riesling*.

• RISOTO DE GÒ •
(Risotto with gobies)

*350 g of rice, 600 g of lagoon gobies, 50 g of butter,
4 spoons of extra-virgin olive oil, 1/2 onion, 1 clove of garlic,
1 glass of dry white wine, 1 glass of wine vinegar,
a few sprigs of parsley, salt, pepper.*

Gobies called "*gò*" in the lagoon, that in the past were one of the principal foods of the lagoon fishermen, are fish with long bodies and characterized by numerous fins; of small size, reaching at the most 15 cm, they are very suitable, other than for the preparation of rice also for the making of excellent fried recipes. Sometimes the rice can be prepared by mixing some *paganéi*, with the *gò*, also little fish that can be bought fresh at the Rialto fish market.

First of all start by cleaning the fish, if it has not already been done by the fishmonger: eliminate the lateral, dorsal and ventral fins using a pair of sharp scissors, shorten the tail, then cut the abdomen from the anal cavity until below the head and empty the fish of its intestinal sac, its intestines and the inner gills, then rinse it under running water and leave it to dry on a clean cloth.

When this operation is complete, salt and pepper the fish slightly and place them in a pan to fry together with the oil, 1/2 a cleaned and chopped onion, a clove of garlic, cleaned and left whole and some chopped parsley.

After having left it for a few minutes on a lively flame, lower it, cover the fish with some warm water and cover with a lid, leaving it to simmer for about half an hour.

When this time has passed; take the fish out of the pan using a spatula with holes, carefully sieve them and obtain a mixture that you will keep warm. Then with as much care as before filter the broth left from the cooking and also leave it aside as it will be needed for the cooking of the rice.

As for the rice, brown the remaining finely chopped onion in butter; add the rice and the hot fish broth a little at a time stirring with a wooden spoon. At half of the cooking time add the *gó* purè, season with salt, add the wine and bring the cooking to an end. If you think it necessary, before serving it, complete with a little butter added after cooking and do not serve too hot.

Do not forget to accompany this delicious risotto with a bottle of fresh, white wine, preferably a *Tocai di Lison* or a *Pinot*.

• RISOTO DE CANÒCE •
(Risotto with mantis shrimps)

350 g of rice, 7 dl of thickened mantis shrimp broth,
50 g of butter, 2 cloves of garlic,
1 small bunch of parsley, pepper.

One can only prepare the risotto with mantis shrimps if you have previously cooked the shrimps and have obtained the broth for the rice.

Then cook the rice in the broth, adding it hot, a little at a time and stirring it with a wooden spoon; cook until ready and finally combine with the butter and season it with some pepper and a mixture of finely chopped garlic and parsley. It should not be necessary to add any salt, but add it eventually after having tasted it.

• RISI E BISÀTO •
(Rice and eel)

*350 g of rice, 1 eel of about 600 g, 1 l of fish fumet
or of vegetable broth, 5 spoons of extra-virgin olive oil,
1 small onion, 1/2 glass of dry, white wine,
2 spoons tomato sauce, salt, pepper.*

Risi e bisàto was once the unfailing and traditional dish for Christmas Eve in Venice. Clean the eel carefully, eliminate the head, dry and cut it into pieces of about 5 cm. Brown the chopped onion in the oil and fry the pieces of eel. When they have changed colour, wet with white wine and let it evaporate, then add the tomato sauce and a little broth and let it simmer for another half hour.

After having salted and peppered it, take the eel out of the pot and keep it in a warm place, all except one small piece, that must be crumbled into the cooking gravy.

Put the pot back on the fire, pour in the rice, stir until it has absorbed the sauce and cook until ready adding the fish fumet or broth a ladle at a time.

Be sure that the rice becomes well dry and lastly serve by laying the pieces of hot eel in the centre of the serving dish and placing the rice around it. Undoubtedly accompany it with some light red wine.

• RISI E BISÀTO CÓ 'L LIMON •
(Rice with lemoned eel)

*350 g of rice, 400 g of eel, 1 l of fish or vegetable broth,
5 spoons of extra-virgin olive oil, 1/2 lemon,
1 clove of garlic, 1 small bunch of parsley,
2 bay leaves, salt, pepper.*

Here we have another version of rice with eel, characterized by the prescence of lemon juice and the perfume of bay leaves, that give this dish a particular flavour.

Firstly clean the eel carefully, eliminate the head and cut it into sections of about 5 cm in length. Pour the oil into a casserole, add some chopped garlic and parsley and let it all brown before adding the eel and salting it slightly. Also add the bay leaves and the lemon juice, thus letting it cook on a moderate flame until two thirds of its cooking span. At this point eliminate the bay leaves and take the pieces of eel out of the casserole so as to be able to easily skin and scale them, then put them back into the container, add the rice and let it all simmer adding the broth a little at a time and mixing it with a wooden spoon.

Once it is finihed cooking, season it with salt and pepper and then serve with a light red wine.

• RISOTO DE SCAMPI •
(Risotto with scampi)

350 g of rice Arborio or dwarf Vialone, 400 g of medium sized scampi (prawns), 1 l of vegetable broth or fish broth, 100 g of butter, 1/2 onion, 1 small bunch of parsley, salt, pepper.

Scampi are considered to be one of the most sought after crustaceans: the flesh, more tender and delicate than that of the lobster, to which family it belongs, is chiefly to be found in the tail. Even though they originate from the north European seas, they are one of the pillars of Venetian cuisine and can be cooked in many ways, one of which uses them to prepare an excellent risotto. They must be very fresh so as to avoid that they may leave a sour taste during cooking. A very popular tradition says that they must be eaten during the months that have the letter R (February, March, April), even though it is difficult to resist their flavour during the rest of the year.

After having shelled them, they must be fried with half the butter and the chopped parsley and flavoured with salt and pepper, while the rice is prepared separately.

For this purpose clean the onion and chop it finely, then fry it in a saucepan with the remaining butter; add the rice and cook it, while adding hot broth a little at a time and stirring with a wooden spoon.

When the rice is almost ready, salt it and add the scampi, stir and leave it on the fire for a few minutes before serving, accompany it with some fresh, white wine, for example a *Tocai di Lison* or a good *Verduzzo*.

• RISOTO DE PEÒCI •
(Risotto with mussels)

350 g of Arborio *rice, 2 kg of* peòci *(mussels),*
less than 1 l of fish broth, 1 small onion, 1 clove of garlic,
5 spoons of extra-virgin olive oil,
1 small bunch of parsley, salt, pepper.

In Venice and surroundings, the word *"peòci"* refers to or-
dinary mussels, traditionally cultivated in the sea that lies
before the city. It is preferable to choose large enough
peòci and it is first of all necessary to eliminate possible
tufts of algae closed between the valves of the mussels,
therefore brush them with a metal or hard bristled brush
then rinse them under running water so as to get rid of
algae and sand and finally wash them with abundantly salted water.

After drying them, put the *peòci* into quite a wide pan and
place it on a lively flame, so that they may open as they
should and release their water.

After about 5 minutes take the pan off the fire and collect
the mussels in a bowl after having extracted them from
the shells; keep their water although you will have to filter
it through a cloth in such a way that you are sure to eliminate every residue of sand.

Keep aside about 20 of the largest and better mussels,
which later you will use to decorate the serving dish, and
commence with the preparation of the risotto.

Clean and chop the onion and the clove of garlic and
brown in a casserole in the oil, then pour in the rice and

let it flavour on a moderate flame, stirring it with a wooden spoon. Add the water of the peòci and when it is finished use the very hot fish broth.

When the rice is almost cooked, salt and pepper to taste,
add the mussels and chopped parsley. Keep it on the flame
for another few minutes and place on the serving plate,
decorate with the *peòci* that you previously kept aside and
serve it not too hot and with the unfailing bottle of fresh,
white wine, a *Tocai di Lison* or a most enjoyable *Riesling*
will be the ideal companions of this dish.

• RISOTO AE CAPESANTE •
(Risotto with scallops)

350 g of rice, 8 scallops, 1.5 l of fish broth, 2 cloves of garlic,
1 small bunch of garden rocket, less than 1 dl of cream,
1/2 glass of dry, white wine, 4 spoons of extra-virgin olive oil,
50 g of butter, salt, pepper.

Scallops, also known as "St. James's shells", are a large type of fan-shaped shell; the inner mollusc is large with consistent flesh. They are present in many recipes, but before
being used they must be adequately cleaned. First of all
they must be brushed and washed carefully, then they must be opened so as to extract the mollusc. If you are not
able to open them when raw, lay them with their convex
side onto the bottom of a pan or on an oven plate and as
soon as they open because of the increasing heat, pry the
hinge between the two valves using a small knife so as to

detach the upper shell. Always using the flexible blade of the knife detatch the "nut" (or white muscle) from either sides and cut the mollusc out. Seperate the "nut" and the coral from the membrane and the fringes that surround them, rinse them under water to free them of the sand, then commence by preparing the garden rocket.

Clean it, grossly chop it and heat it in the oil in which you have first browned a clove of chopped garlic. After a few minutes take it off the flame and chop it all with a crescent-shaped chopping knife or simply blend it together with the cream, then salt and pepper and put the sauce back on the fire for a few minutes, so that it may sufficiently thicken.

Bring the broth to the boil and scald the scallops for a few instances, then turn it off leaving the molluscs inside.

In a pot soften in butter the remaining clean and finely chopped clove of garlic, pour in the rice and toast il well in the condiment. Wet with the white wine and, as soon as it has evaporated, cook the rice adding, one at a time, a ladle of broth from which you have removed the scallops.

Lastly, amalgamate the rocket cream together with the rice and the scallops cut into strips, then turn it off. Leave it to cream for a few minutes and finally serve it without forgetting to open a bottle of good, fresch, white wine, for example a *Tocai di Lison* that also in this case seems particulary indicated to revive the dinner table.

• RISOTO AE CAPESANTE •
(Risotto with scallops)

• RISOTO AI SARDÓNI •
(Risotto with anchovies)

350 g of rice, 8 salted herrings, 1 l of fish or vegetable broth,
1 small onion, 1 carrot, 1 celery stalk,
1 small bunch of parsley, grated parmesan cheese,
extra-virgin olive oil as needed, pepper.

As everybody knows, the anchovy, small fish that rarely surpasses the length of 15 cm, lends itself to being cooked in various ways and to being conserved - in oil, in salt and even smoked. Its use also consents the preparation of an excellent risotto, that is cooked without any difficulty and few expenses. Firstly clean the vegetables and chop them finely, then brown them in a few spoons of oil after having poured them into the casserole. Keep stirring them with a wooden spoon and after a few minutes of cooking add the rice and let it toast, without stopping to stir it.

Then add the hot filtered broth, a ladle at a time.

Meanwhile clean the salt off the anchovies and keep one aside; then prepare a sauce by pressing the anchovies in a small pan in which you have heated some oil.

Amalgamate the anchovy sauce with the rice when it has reached half of its cooking span and, just before taking it off the flame, add the finely chopped parsley, a few spoons of grated parmesan cheese, some ground pepper and the anchovy that was kept aside and grossly chopped. After having turned it off, leave it to thicken for a few minutes before serving it with an unfailing bottle of fresh, dry, white wine.

• In-between dishes •

> *Gran risi!*
> *E quela sopa?*
> *La carne era squsita.*
> *Che castrà! Che fritura! Mi ghe andava de vita.*
> *Quele quatro moleche no gièrele perfete?*
> *I s'ha desmentegà de tagiarghe le ongiete.*
>
> (Carlo Goldoni, *I morbinosi*, 1758-59)

Here we have the real triumph of seafood cuisine: from cooking in the oven to the grill, from fried to boiled to stewed recipies. There is one for every taste: cheap and more expensive fish, molluscs, crustaceans, to be bought very fresh and eaten with the suitable accompaniments of vegetables and wines.

• SÉPE CÓ'L TÒCIO NÉRO •
(Cuttlefish in black)

700 g of cuttlefish, 1 onion, 1 clove of garlic,
less than 1/2 glass of extra-virgin olive oil, 1 bay leaf
1 lemon rind, 1 glass of dry, white wine,
nutmeg, salt, pepper.

Carefully clean the cuttlefish. First of all eliminate the blackish skin that covers it, then cut along the back lengthwise using a small, sharp knife. Opening the cut, extract the bone which is as long as the whole body of the mollusc, being careful not to break open the ink sac.

Using a finger, extract the intestinal sac and from it detach the ink sac and keep it aside. Then separate the tentacles from the sac below the eyes that must also be taken off. Between the tentacles you will find the beak, or rostrum, that must also be eliminated.

Rinse it under running water and let it dry on a cloth.

Peel and chop the onion and garlic, let them brown in the oil which was poured in the casserole, add the cuttlefish which was cut into strips of about a couple of centimetres each, season with salt and freshly ground pepper, add the bay leaf, the lemon rind and a pinch of powdered nutmeg. Stir, also add the ink diluted in wine and let it simmer on a moderate flame, letting the sauce thicken, stirring it now and then with a wooden spoon.

Leave it on the fire for a time span which, according to the consistency of the cuttlefish, can vary between 40 and 60 minutes; if however, the molluscs are not sufficiently

tender, do not be afraid to lengthen the cooking time.
Serve with a good, steaming polenta and a fresh, white wine: a *Tocai* or a *Pinot grigio* are very indicated.

• SEPIOÌNE IN UMIDO •
(Small, stewed cuttlefish)

*1 kg of small cuttlefish, 1 large onion, 1 clove of garlic,
1 glass of fish or vegetable broth, 1 glass of white wine,
a few spoonsful of tomato sauce, extra-virgin olive oil,
1 small bunch of parsley, salt, pepper.*

Carefully clean the cuttlefish keeping aside the small ink
sacs, cutting the larger ones into small strips.
In a large pan pour abundant oil and brown the cleaned

and chopped onion and the clean and pressed clove of garlic, that you will take out as soon as it browns. Add the small cuttlefish and let them cook for about 10 minutes before wetting with wine and letting it evaporate.

As soon as the wine has evaporated pour the fish or vegetable broth into the pan, in which you have dissolved the ink sacs which were kept aside, add the tomato sauce, salt, pepper and leave it on the fire for about half an hour.

Once the cooking is terminated, sprinkle it with chopped parsley and finally serve it together with some maize porridge (*polenta*) and a bottle of fresh, white wine.

• SEPIOÌNE IN UMIDO •
(Small, stewed cuttlefish)

• CAEAMÀRI FRITI •
(Small, fried calamari)

500 g of small calamari, wheat flour as needed,
extra-virgin olive oil as needed, salt.
<u>To garnish:</u> 2 lemons.

The calamari is a mollusc that lends itself to the preparation of multiple recipes, the smaller it is, the more tender it is and, as for the carrying out of this recipe, it is preferable to use small specimens.

Start by cleaning the molluscs, seperate the tentacles from the rest of the body so as to let the entrails out that will remain attached to the head; empty the sac from the eventual residue, wash it under running water and free it from the internal membranes and the external skin; push back the sac until you identify the "feather" - a type of bone which has the shape of a small, long and flexible blade - and extract it by pulling delicately; clean the tuft of tentacles from the head and from the entrails that were left attached and eliminate the beak. Then dry them and put them through the flour and fry them in a pan in which there is enough oil. Do not let them over-cook as they risk becoming hard, other than loosing their flavour - which would really be a pity. When they have cooked to the right point, take them out of the pan, leave them to dry of the excess oil on absorbent kitchen paper and finally salt and serve them with a lemon cut into wedges, so that each table companion may flavour them as he wishes.

Do not forget to open a bottle of fresh, dry, white wine.

• MULLET FROM MURANO •

*700 g of gutted mullet, extra-virgin olive oil,
white wine vinegar, 3 bay leaves, salt.*

There are those who cook mullet without gutting it, giving
the fish a particular flavour; therefore you may eventually
experiment this method. In any case, proceed to accurately scale the fish, wash it under running water and dry it
before placing it on the oven plate or in a pan, wet it
with abundant oil, sprinkle it with vinegar and salt it. If
the fish has been gutted, put the bay leaves into the cavity.
Place it in a hot oven and keeping the temperature of
about 170 °C leave it to cook for about half an hour,
without forgetting to sprinkle the fish with a little vinegar
when it has reached half of its cooking time.
Finally serve it hot with some slices of polenta toasted on
the plate.

• SARDÈE IMPANAE 1 •
(Pilchard cutlets)

*16 fresh pilchards, 1 egg, maize seed oil,
grated bread as needed, salt.*
<u>*To garnish:*</u> *2 lemons, salad.*

Here is another way to use pilchards, a very cheap fish
which in its simplicity is able to satisfy many needs. Pilchard cutlets, an irresistible dish, are prepared in a very

easy way; first of all take the head off each fish and, after having opened it lengthwise, eliminate the bones but not the tail. You will obtain a cutlet with two flat and joined fillets that you will pass through the grated bread after having wetted them with salted, beaten egg. Then pour the oil into a suitable pan and fry the cutlets until they have acquired a pleasing golden colour, after this take them out of the pan using a skimming spoon and leave them for a few minutes in the warmth on absorbent kitchen paper so as to get rid of the excess grease.

Finally serve them hot, decorating the plate with small slices of lemon and fresh salad of the season, accompany with fresh, dry white wine.

• SARDÈE IMPANAE 2 •
(Pilchard cutlets)

16 fresh pilchards, 2 eggs, maize seed oil,
wheat flour as needed, salt.
<u>*To garnish:*</u> *1 lemon, salad.*

It is nothing other than a simple variant of the Pilchard cutlet's recipe, in which instead of using the grated bread one uses flour.

Take the head off each fish and, after cutting it lengthwise, eliminate the bones but not the tail. You will obtain a cutlet of two flat and joined fillets, that you will pass through the flour after wetting them in a plate of beaten and salted eggs.

Pour some oil into a suitable pan and fry the fillets until they have become a nice golden colour, after this take them out of the pan, using a skimming spoon and leave them on some absorbent kitchen paper so that they may loose the excess grease. Finally serve them hot with slices of lemon and fresh salad of the season, accompany with a fresh, dry, white wine, and if you think it necessary, with some steaming white maize porridge (*polenta*).

• SARDÈE CÓ 'L PARSÉMOLO •
(Pilchards with parsley)

500 g of small sized pilchards,
1/2 glass of extra-virgin olive oil,
2 cloves of garlic, parsley, salt, pepper.

Clean the pilchards by eliminating the head and entrails, wash and let them dry on a clean kitchen towel.

Pour the oil into a pan, heat it, add an abundant mixture of chopped garlic and parsley and let it cook, wetting it all with 1/2 a glass of water and stirring it with a wooden spoon; then season it with salt and freshly ground pepper. Lower the flame, add the pilchards and let them cook for about 10 minutes with the lid off the pan. Finally serve hot and with a dry, white and unfailingly fresh wine.

• STORIÓN AEA GRÈA •
(Grilled sturgeon)

800 g of sturgeon, extra-virgin olive oil as needed,
2 cloves of garlic,
1 bay leaf, a few sprigs of parsley, salt, pepper.

Once the sturgeon, a fish that can reach remarkable sizes, was common to the Adriatic sea and would swim upstream in springtime and at the beginning of summer, so as to lay the eggs and was therefore caught and cooked quite often.

● SARDÈE CÓ 'L PARSÉMOLO ●
(Pilchards with parsley)

The excessive increase of water pollution has made the presence of this fish quite rare.

It has fat and consistent flesh and can be cooked in sections or cutlets, on the grill or in the oven; it is excellent also when eaten raw, cut into very thin strips that are pickled before using them for delicious starters.

Cut the sturgeon into four sections, eliminate the skin, season it with some freshly ground pepper and place the chunks to marinade for about ten minutes in the oil flavoured with peeled and chopped garlic and the bay leaf.

Passed the given time, take the chunks out of the marinade, drain them, and place them onto the grill, flavouring them with salt and turning them, so that they may grill on either side.

Once the cooking is ultimated, dust them with some chopped parsley and wet them with a drop of oil.

• ORAE AEA GRÈA •
(Grilled giltheads)

4 medium sized giltheads, extra-virgin olive oil,
salt and pepper.

According to its dimensions, the gilthead can be cooked whole on the grill, fried (when dealing with a small specimen) or in the oven as fillets. It is a very appreciated fish by the Venetians, particularly on important occasions.

After having washed, scaled and gutted the giltheads, let

them rest for at least an hour in a marinade of oil, salt and pepper. Then brush the grill with some oil, heat it and place the giltheads on it to cook, greasing them now and again with the marinade and turning them a couple of times during the cooking span.

Finally serve with salad and a fresh, dry, white wine.

• BRANSÍN AL FORNO •
(Baked bass)

*2 bass of about 500 g, 2 onions, 4 ripe tomatoes,
2 lemons, exrta-virgin olive oil, salt, pepper.*

Bass also called "spigola" is a fish with exceptional meat, white and consistent, that the Venetians usually prepare as tradition on Christmas Eve but also, especially in recent times, for the Old Year's Eve dinner. If of small size, it can be cooked whole or boiled, otherwise it is better to cut it into pieces.

First of all start by cleaning the fish, that must obviously be very fresh: after having gutted them (an operation that must be done at once after buying it or even at the moment you buy it), wash and dry them with a clean cloth. Then wet an oven pan with some oil and lay the clean onions, sliced into rings, covering them with the tomatoes cut into very thin slices. Then lay the fish on the vegetables, season with salt and pepper, wet with a drop of oil and complete with the lemons cut into small slices.

After having placed it in the oven at a middle temperature, leave it to cook for about half an hour and then serve it accompanied by vegetables and a bottle of good, white and moderately fresh wine.

• BRANSÍN LÉSO •
(Boiled bass)

1 bass of 1.5 kg in weight, 1 lemon, 1 celery stalk,
2 bay leaves, extra-virgin olive oil, salt, pepper in granules.

Get some very fresh bass, gut it immediately or even ask your fishmonger to do so the moment you buy it, then scale it, take off the gills and wash it well under cold, running water. Get a fish kettle, a special pot furnished with a grill for cooking fish, and place the bass inside, cover it with water, salt it and add half a lemon, the bay leaves, the washed celery stalk and the pepper in granules. Place the pot on the fire, bring to boil and let it do so for 15 minutes, adjust the flame so that the water just boils and the cooking becomes "sweet" in such a way that the fish does no break.

Once the cooking is done, take the bass out of the container and see that you eliminate the head, the bones and the fins.

Then place it on a serving dish, garnish it with small slices of lemon and flavour it with oil, a little salt and a dusting of freshly ground pepper, serving it together with a bottle of white wine.

• CAPESANTE FRITE •

(Fried scallops)

12 scallops, 2 eggs, 1/2 cup of grated bread,
a little white wheat flour, 3 dl of extra-virgin olive oil,
1 spoon of chopped parsley.

To start, brush and wash the shell of every scallop and then using a kitchen cloth, hold it tightly with your left hand in such a way that the flat shell is facing upwards and the joining point is facing outwards. With your right hand stick the blade of a small knife into a crack between the two valves and with a jerking movement pry them without breaking them, working your way up to the joining point and cutting the muscles that keep the mollusc anchored to the valves. If this operation is too difficult, place the shells in a very moderately heated oven, so that the valves may open them without difficulty.

Once the shell is open, slip the blade under the greyish external border (the "cloak") so as to detach the mollusc.

Divide the "nut" (white muscle) and the coral from the rest that must be discarded, eventually keeping the "cloak", that can be used for the preparation of fish, broths and fumets. Lastly rinse the molluscs under water and dry them.

Beat the egg in a bowl, salt it and then dip the scallops into it, after which slightly flour them and pass them through the grated bread poured out on a plate.

Heat the oil in a large pan and, when it is very hot, fry the molluscs for just two or three minutes and then transfer them onto some absorbent kitchen paper, so that they may get rid of the excess grease.

Finally put the molluscs back into the shells that you kept aside, decorate with a bit of chopped parsley and serve with a good, fresh, white wine, for example a *Tocai di Lison* or a *Prosecco*.

• CANESTRÈI FRITI •
(Fried "canestrelli")

700 g of canestrelli, wheat flour as needed,
1 dl of maize seed oil, salt
<u>*To garnish:*</u> *1 lemon.*

"Canestrelli" are the little brothers of the scallops or St. James's shell, which look alike, both in the shape of the valves, even though they are much smaller and in the structure of the mollusc. They are generally sold already shelled and can be used in a mixed fry;

if absolutely sure of their freshness, they can also be eaten raw, flavoured with oil and lemon juice. The specimens that are gathered in the lagoon normally have a more consistent flesh than those of the sea.

Carefully wash the canestrelli in cold water, turning them a few times with your hands so that may discard the sand. Once you have concluded this operation, flour them.

Then heat the oil in a pan and pour the canestrelli in, leaving them to fry until a characteristic sizzling announces a satisfactory completion.

At this point, take them out of the pan using a skimming spoon and lay them for a few minutes on some absorbent, kitchen paper, salt them and shake the paper. Finally pour them onto a serving dish, garnish them with small slices of lemon and serve them with white wine, a *Tocai di Lison*.

• SIÉVOLI AL FORNO •
(Baked grey mullet)

4 grey mullets of 200 g each, about 10 bay leaves,
10 spoons of extra-virgin olive oil, wine vinegar, salt.

There are numerous types of grey mullet with similar meat, a bit fatty but delicate and soft that lend themselves to be cooked in many ways, in the oven, on the grill, or roasted.

The eating habits of this fish greatly influence the flavour of the meat: if it originates from seas which are oxygenated and not polluted, the meat will be of an excellent kind; if instead it comes from polluted areas, the quality will greatly deteriorate, even to the point of having to throw everything away.

With regards to the recipe, first of all scale the fish, gut them, wash them carefully and then lay them in a pan, preferably of terracotta, after having placed bay leaves on the bottom. Sprinkle them with oil and vinegar, salt them and place them in a preheated oven which is not too hot, letting them cook for 40 minutes. After this time control the cooking and finally serve with a steaming maize porridge (*polenta*) and accompany with a bottle of light, red wine.

• SIÉVOLO RÓSTO •
(Grilled grey mullet)

4 grey mullets of 200 g each, extra-virgin olive oil, lemon juice, salt, pepper.

First of all get some very fresh fish, scale them, gut them, wash them carefully and to complete the operation let them marinade for at least an hour in a container with oil, lemon juice, salt and pepper.

After the given time, grease the grill with a little oil, place the mullets on top and let them cook for about half an hour, brushing them now and then with the marinade. Finally serve together with some salad and a fresh white wine, a *Prosecco* for example.

• GÒ IN BROÉTO •
(Gobies in broth)

*750 g of lagoon gobies, 2 cloves of garlic,
1 glass of extra-virgin olive oil, 1/2 glass of white wine,
1/2 glass of wine vinegar, salt, pepper.*

Carefully clean the fish, eliminating the entrails and wash them very well without scaling. Pour the oil into a casserole, heat it, add the clean garlic cloves and, when they start to darken, eliminate them and place the fish into the container.

Salt and pepper them, add the wine, the vinegar and enough water to partly cover them. After having placed a lid onto it but leaving it slightly open, leave it to cook for about 20 minutes, increasing the cooking time if dealing with relatively large fish.

Finally serve with some slices of toasted maize porridge (*polenta*), without leaving out a good white wine.

Once not long ago, fishermen would cook *gò* directly on their boats, without the addition of any type of fat, only with some sea water; in the sauce that would form at the bottom of the cooking container, they would dip the slices of polenta.

• RÉNGA AI FÉRI •
(Grilled herrings)

*4 salted and smoked herrings, milk, extra-virgin olive oil,
a few sprigs of parsley, 1 clove of garlic.*

The *rénga* was once the queen of Lent in the whole of Veneto and in some ways this tradition still exists, as in the "herring festivals" that take place in certain towns on Ash Wednesday and are a residue of that custom when the last ones to wear masks and the night wanderers of Shrove Tuesday would return home carrying a herring on a bamboo stick, that would symbolize the abstinence from meat while awaiting the Easter Ressurrection. Herring was once prepared in many and simple ways and was a fish that could be served in the humblest of homes, seeing that it was affordable to every pocket.

As for the recipe, boil the herrings in water and milk for a few minutes, then take them out of the pot, let them dry and then place them onto the grill. Let them cook well, scale them, divide them into fillets and lay them in a bowl. Cover them with oil, chopped parsley and garlic and let them marinade in a cool place for a couple of days.

Finally serve with some toasted polenta and a bottle of some excellent *Tocai di Lison* or a just as enjoyable *Pinot grigio*.

• RÉNGA CÓEA POÉNTA BRUSTOEÀDA •
(Herring with toasted polenta)

4 salted and smoked herrings, milk, extra-virgin olive oil,
a few sprigs of parsley, 1 clove of garlic, pepper.

Open and clean the herrings, cut them into fillets and boil
them in milk and water for little more than 5 minutes.
Let them cool, take them out of the pot, let them dry
well and put them in a bowl.
Flavour them with a mixture of chopped garlic and parsley
and with a dusting of freshly ground pepper, cover them
with oil and let them marinade for a few hours before serving them with some hot toasted maize porridge (polenta)
and some white wine, possibly with a *Tocai di Lison*, to be
enjoyed fresh.

• COA DE ROSPO CÒE PATATE •
(Angler fish with potatoes)

800 g of angler fish, salt.
<u>*To go with it:*</u> *400 g of potatoes, extra-virgin olive oil,*
lemon, 1 small bunch of parsley, salt.

The head, large and unproportioned in comparison to the
body, together with its numerous teeth and its useles-
sness other than to prepare excellent fish soups, makes
the angler fish or "pescatrice" a miniature sea monster.
However it has tasty and consistent meat with a delicate

taste that makes it one of the most sought after fish by connoisseurs, who do not deny that it is on a par with lobster and "granceola". Generally it is sold already with the head taken off.

As for the recipe, it is absolutely simple to prepare, it is sufficient to boil the angler fish in salted water for about half an hour, drain it well and serve it on a serving dish. An excellent accompaniment is that of a side dish of boiled potatoes sprinkled with chopped parsley; furthermore, do not forget to serve with some lemon wedges and some good quality oil with which one can flavour the potatoes and the fish.

There are even those who do not despise the use of mayonnaise as a condiment; if you like the idea, prepare it at home. In any case, do not forget to choose the right wine that must be unfailingly white and enjoyably fresh.

• COA DE ROSPO IN UMIDO •
(Stewed angler fish)

4 chunks of angler fish 200 g each, 250 g of ripe tomatoes,
1 onion, 1 celery stalk, 1 clove of garlic,
6 spoons of extra-virgin olive oil,
a few sprigs of parsley, salt, pepper.

The first thing to do when preparing this recipe is to dedicate oneself to the preparation of the tomatoes that will serve to flavour the fish.

You will therefore have to skin them after having dropped

them for a moment in boiling water and eliminate the seeds and sieve. Then clean the slices of angler fish.

Completed these operations, clean and chop the parsley and then fry the lot in a saucepan in which you have poured the oil, then add the fish, fry them on either side, salt and pepper them. Lower the flame, add the tomato pulp and let it simmer for 20 minutes, that should be sufficient for a satisfactory cooking. Finally salt and pepper to taste and serve accompanied by some fresh, white wine.

• Fiéti de Sanpièro Impanài •
(John Dory fillet cutlets)

500 g of John Dory fish fillets, 150 g of butter,
1 egg, wheat flour, grated bread, salt.
<u>*To garnish:*</u> *2 lemons*

Of unmistakable aspect, a large head, a long and spiney dorsal fin, a very flat and oval body, the John Dory fish has a characteristic round black spot on each side and reaches a medium weight of about one and a half kilograms. The white and consistent meat, without many bones, is similar to that of turbot and sole and can be cooked in the same way.

As for the carrying out of this recipe, it is useful to remember that usually the John Dory fish is sold already cut into fillets.

To start, wash the fillets, dry them well and then flour and wet them in a plate with salted, beaten egg; finally dip them in bread crumbs on either side. Put the butter in a pan, let it melt and fry the fillets on a moderate flame, letting them become a golden brown. Do not be hasty because they are normally of a thick consistency.

Finally transfer them onto a serving dish, garnish with lemon wedges and serve them without leaving out a bottle of excellent, fresh, dry, white wine such as a *Tocai di Lison*.

• MOÉCHE FRITE •
(Fried crab)

*600 g of moéche, 4 eggs, extra-virgin olive oil,
wheat flour as needed, salt.*

Moéche are small crabs of the Venetian lagoon that are traditionally served in spring, at the time of the year in which they change their shells, they are soft and therefore suitable for consumption without having to clean them, that owing to their size would be nearly impossible. The preparation of this dish reveals a certain insensitivity towards the "torture" that these molluscs must undergo, but so it is.

Moéche in fact are bought live or at least very fresh and, after having washed them several times, they are immersed in a bowl in which the eggs have been beaten and salted. Then immerse the small crabs for a couple of hours so that they - litterally - drown in the beaten egg (it is recommended to cover the container with a lid and place a weight on top). Then eliminate the ends of the legs, put them through the flour and fry in a pan with plenty of oil. When they have become a pleasing golden colour, salt and transfer them onto a serving dish, ready to be served with a good steaming polenta and accompanied by a bottle of good fresh, white wine.

Using the fried *moéche*, one can eventually prepare an excellent omelette. In that case, it is necessary to grossly chop them, combine them with other beaten eggs and finally cook the omelette in a large frying pan.

DRY SALTED COD AND STOCKFISH

As everybody knows, dry, salted cod is nothing other than cod which has been decapitated, opened and preserved in salt. Its name probably derives from the Spanish word *bacalao* (that has the same meaning) and this word probably also derives from the old Dutch word *bakkeljauw* or *kabeljauw* or maybe from the Romance *cabilh* ("chief").

Before using it one must clean the salt of it carefully, washing it under running water and then leaving it to soak in a basin, often renewing the water or better still placing the container under a tap of trickling water. One can also buy the so called "wet cod", that does not need such preliminary operations and is ready for use after a necessary wash under cold water.

• BACAEÀ RÓSTO •
(Baked dry salted cod)

800 g of boned and soaked dry salted cod, 3 large onions,
wheat flour as needed, 8 dl of extra-virgin olive oil,
8 dl of milk, 1 glass of dry white wine,
1 small bunch of parsley, nutmeg, salt, pepper.

Wash and dry the cod, cut it into sections of nearly equal size and pass it well through the flour.

Peel the onions, cut half of them into very thin slices and lay them on the bottom of a terracotta pot, not treated

Stockfish is instead decapitated cod, opened and dried traditionally in the wind and sun; it must be adequately softened before cooking and for this reason must be beaten with a wooden bat and left to soak for 3-4 days, regulary changing the water and leaving it in a basin under a tap of trickling water, although it is possible to buy it ready-beaten and soaked.

Even the origin of the word "stockfish" is nordic: in fact, in old Dutch we have the word *stokvish* where stok means stick and *vish* fish, therefore stick-fish or better still fish dried on sticks.

Fish that on its own is rather insipid, tough and stringy, cod can be prepared in many ways that allows one to obtain a very tasty dish and it is just this that the traditional Venetian cuisine was able to create.

with toxic paints, add a quarter of the oil and the cod on top; also finely slice the remaning onions, use them to cover the cod and season with salt, pepper and nutmeg. Sprinkle with another quarter of the oil and place the pot in the fire letting it brown on a moderate flame. After a while, pour the wine and continue cooking on a very moderate flame, adding the milk a little at a time, that must be absorbed almost completely.

Let it cook for another 90 minutes, then add the other quarter of oil and transfer the pan into the preheated oven, letting it cook at a moderate heat.

Every now and then move the pieces of cod without mixing them and wet them with the gravy from the bottom of the pot.

The moment you serve it, add the remaining oil and chopped parsley serving it together with steaming polenta and some good, dry, white wine, for example a freshly uncorked *Pinot bianco* or a *Tocai di Lison*.

• BACAEÀ IN TÉCIA •
(Dry salted cod in the pan)

800 g of soaked and boned dry salted cod,
40 g of salted anchovies, 1 large onion, wheat flour as needed,
2.5 dl extra-virgin olive oil, 1 spoon of salted capers, 100 g
of grated parmesan cheese, 1 small bunch of parsley, salt, pepper.

Wash and dry the cod carefully, cut it into equal sized pieces and pass it through some flour, so as to "whiten" it

● BACAEÀ IN TÉCIA ●
(Dry salted cod in the pan)

as it should be. Pour the oil into a pan, add the peeled and finely sliced onion, the desalted anchovies, the rinsed capers, the milk, cover it with a suitable lid and leave to cook on a low flame for about three hours, checking now and then that the pieces of cod do not stick to the bottom, moving them delicately with a wooden spoon.

Control the cooking, salt and pepper to taste, dust it with the parsley, leave to rest for a moment, then bring to table. Accompany it with some polenta and serve with some fresh, dry, white wine. An excellent suggestion is a *Tocai di Lison* or a *Pinot grigio*.

• BISÀTO IN UMIDO 1 •
(Stewed eel)

800 g of small eels, wheat flour as needed,
4 spoons of extra-virgin olive oil,
2 cloves of garlic, less than 1 glass of dry, white wine,
1/2 spoon of tomato puree, a few sprigs of parsley, salt, pepper.

Eel is easily caught and has always been considered a nutritious meat: its pulp is very tasty and fatty, not always easily digestible, it must be cooked very carefully because its blood in the raw state is toxic.

Clean the eels, wash them and cut them into small sections of 5-6 centimetres in length. Flour them by passing them through the flour which has been poured onto a plate and brown them in a pan with oil, together with the peeled and pressed garlic cloves and the chopped parsley.

● BISÀTO IN UMIDO ●
(Stewed eel)

After browning them, properly add the wine, flavour with salt and fresh pepper, combine the tomato puree, let it cook on a moderate flame and bring the cooking to an end.

Before serving, salt to taste, accompany it with some toasted maize porridge (*polenta*) and some red wine, for example a *Merlot di Pramaggiore*, or with a dry, white wine.

• BISÀTO IN UMIDO 2 •
(Stewed eel)

800 g of eel, 1 medium sized onion, 1 clove of garlic,
a little wheat flour, 3 spoons of extra-virgin olive oil,
20 g of butter, 1 glass of wine vinegar,
1 glass of dry white wine,
3 peeled tomatoes, 1 spoon of chopped parsley, salt, pepper.

After having rubbed the eel with maize flour, some coarse salt or some grated bread, take out the entrails and leave to soak in water and vinegar for about half an hour. Meanwhile peel the onion and the garlic and chop them finely. After the soaking time has passed, place the oil and butter into a saucepan and brown the chopped onion and garlic: when it starts darkening, add the eel which has been cut into sections of 5-6 cm and pass them though the flour poured on a plate.

Leave it to brown slightly, then turn it with a wooden spoon, add the white wine, let it evaporate and straight afterwards add the peeled and seeded tomatoes.

Continue cooking until 2/3 of its cooking time, about 15 minutes, salt to taste season with some freshly ground pepper and bring the cooking to an end under the cover of a lid.

Finally add chopped parsley, mixed delicately and serve with yellow maize porridge (*polenta*).

• BISÀTO FRITO 1 •
(Fried eel)

700 g of eel, 2 onions, 1 carrot, 100 g of butter,
1 glass of dry white wine, 3 egg yolks, 1 cup of grated bread,
3 spoons of wheat flour, 1 bay leaf,
1 clove, thyme, salt, pepper.
For frying: extra-virgin olive oil and maize seed oil.

First of all, skin the eel and then cut it into sections of about 10 cm each. Put the pieces into a baking-pan, add the white wine, the onions cleaned and cut in slices, the carrot cleaned and cut into rings, the bay leaf and a bit of thyme, a knob of butter, the crumbled clove, salt, pepper and let it all cook for about 20 minutes on a moderate flame.

After the given time has passed, take the pieces of eel out of the container and prepare seperately a sauce by combining on the flame, the remaining butter, the flour, the eel's cooking gravy and, after a few minutes of cooking, the egg yolks. Consider the sauce ready when it has been on the fire for about 10 minutes and then let it cool before dipping in the pieces of eel and then passing them through grated bread on a plate.

To complete, fry the eel in a pan in which you have poured sufficient oil, the take out the pieces with a skimming spoon and transfer them onto a plate on which you have layed some absorbent kitchen paper. Finally serve accompanying them with a bottle of red wine, for example a Merlot di Pramaggiore uncorked at 16-18 °C.

• BISÀTO FRITO 2 •
(Fried eel)

800 g of eel, wheat flour as needed, salt.
For frying: extra-virgin olive oil, maize seed oil.

Gut a couple of eels, eliminate the heads, cut them lengthwise and then into small chunks of 5 to 6 cm in length. Flour the small pieces passing them through the flour on a plate and then fry them in boiling oil that was poured into a pan. When they have cooked to the right point, transfer them onto some absorbent kitchen paper, salt them and keep them in the warmth until the moment of serving with toasted polenta and some good, red wine, for example a *Merlot di Pramaggiore*.

• BISÀTO RÓSTO •
(Baked eel)

700 g of eel, plenty of bay leaves, salt, pepper.

The fatty and consistent meat of the eel lends itself perfectly to oven baking and in fact it is one of the traditional ways of cooking in the Venetian lagoon.

After having cleaned and decapitated them, cut the eel into pieces of about 5 cm in length and place them in a baking-pan on top of a layer of very perfumed fresh bay leaves putting the pieces close to one another but avoiding any contact. Salt and pepper to taste, pour a little water into the container and after having preheated the oven to a medium temperature, place the pan inside and let the pieces of eel cook until they become tender enough (now and then prick with a fork, so as to feel to what point the cooking has arrived).

Finally serve directly in the cooking container and, if possible, serve it with maize porridge (*polenta*) and an unfailing bottle of red wine suitable for this dish. If your choice is a good *Merlot di Pramaggiore*, you will certainly not be sorry.

• BIBLIOGRAPHY •

AGOSTINI, P. - ZORZI, A. *A tavola con i Dogi*, Arsenale, Venice, 1991.

ALBERINI, A., *L'antica cucina veneziana*, Piemme, Casale Monferrato, 1990.

BRUSEGAN, M., *La cucina veneziana*, Newton & Compton, Rome, 1997.

DA MOSTO, R., *Il Veneto in cucina*, Giunti Martello, Florence, 1974.

MAFFIOLI, G., *La cucina veneziana*, Muzzio, Padua, 1982.

MARANGONI, G., *Proverbi di casa nostra*, Filippi, Venice, 1995.

MILANI, M. (a cura di), *Massime e proverbi Goldoniani,* Editoriale Programma, Padua, 1993.

SALVATORI DE ZULIANI, *A tola co i nostri veci. La cucina veneziana*, Angeli, Milan, 1986.

SCHIAFFINO, M. (a cura di), *Venezia in cucina Mondadori*, Milan, 1994.

ZARDO M. - BRANDIS, J., *Bàccari a Venezia. Mangiare a bere a Venezia*, Frasnelli - Keitsch, Bolzano, 1994.

• INDEX •

Last printed in August 1998
by Grafiche BUSTI S.r.l-Colognola ai Colli (VR)
DEMETRA S.r.l.